The Simple Truths
of Selling

The most important things you should know.

By Todd Duncan

Published by Simple Truths
1952 McDowell Road, Suite 300
Naperville, IL 60563

Design: Rich Nickel : Cover by John Vieceli
Printed and bound in the United States of America

www.simpletruths.com

ISBN: 978-1-60810-146-7

01 WOZ 12

Contents

Introduction

A couple years ago my team did a little research and figured out that in the United States alone, one in every twenty-three people is a salesperson. That statistic, while already remarkable, becomes almost startling when you consider that it doesn't subtract out people who don't work, who are retired, or who are still in diapers. In other words, the real statistic—removing those who are not employed in any way—is probably that approximately one in every four working adults in the U.S. is a salesperson.

It would stand to reason then, that competition is everywhere you turn in this profession. And to make the odds of succeeding even tougher, we generally pull from the same didactic pot of information. We read the same bestsellers and blogs, browse the same trendy websites and listen to the same sales trainers. There are exceptions of course, but for the general learning majority this is true.

As a result, the challenge in writing books on selling is mastering the art of saying something new without ignoring what is popular. Unfortunately, the nature of the beast is that, as an author, you can only rarely break free from what salespeople are already reading and still sell a couple hundred thousand books. That is, of course, unless you are saying something that is impervious to trends. That is what we hope to accomplish with this book.

In the following pages, you won't find new, breakthrough theories on selling. Then again, if you were taught wrong from the beginning, some of the ideas may seem quite revolutionary. Nevertheless, what you will find in the following pages are lucid descriptions of the foundational truths of selling that endow any salesperson with success, no matter their product or industry.

Much of what we are taught about successful selling these days is overstated and it causes us to forget the fundamental precepts that make selling what it should be—a tool that brings people the solutions they seek. The paradox of sales training is that the more methodology we learn, the less authentic we seem, and the less successful we tend to be.

In light of all that's been said and will be said about how to sell well, it would behoove us to maintain, at the core of our endeavors, the simple truths of successful selling that rarely ever change. They are what this book is about.

As you read the stories and descriptions, view the pictures, and consider the provoking quotes, let the combination of them speak to you and teach you. Absorb their lessons and ask yourself one question: "Do I maintain this simple truth in my selling?" Your answers will most certainly be yes—at times. But when you, being gut-honest, have to admit that your answer is not yes, then the learning has really begun.

Don't let this book become only an entertainment to you (though I hope it serves that purpose in part). Let this book become a regular reference—an accountability partner of sorts who reminds you of the fundamental goals of selling and, when necessary, nudges you back on track. If you allow this book to serve that purpose, I am confident that you will be regularly and readily equipped to meet the needs of your customers. And the better you are at that, the more successful you will become.

Todd Duncan

Prospects
should be
expecting
you.

My orientation into professional selling consisted of, "Here's your desk; here's your phone; good luck Todd, you're on your own." I was lost from the start.

I was given a territory that stretched thirty miles and within it were twenty-five key accounts with whom I was to develop a business relationship. I was a mortgage originator and these accounts were real estate agencies who would, in theory, want to use my services to secure financing for their home-buying clients. I learned quickly that theories are often not realities.

I walked through the front door of that first building and immediately everyone became busy. They picked up their phones feigning an important call or started talking with coworkers—anything to dodge an encounter with me, who clearly wore "Salesperson" on my forehead.

To get to the point, nothing happened. No contacts, no prospects, no sales. I drove to the next agency and got the same result. And the next and the next. After five rejections, I quit and went to the beach. It was sunny.

While my decision didn't demonstrate the best work ethic, quitting that day ended up being a wise move. After some thinking time on the sand, I called a friend in the real estate business and asked if I could observe how my peers were selling to the people in his office. He agreed and I spent the next three hours cringing at the same mistakes I made. Then, at about 4:00 P.M., a pleasant face with a leather portfolio strolled through the door. He asked for a woman by name and within seconds he was in her office. Forty-five minutes later, she escorted him to the front door and in parting he said, "Thanks for your time. I look forward to a long and profitable partnership." My heart felt warm again. He had it and I wanted it.

The man's name was John and I connected with him shortly thereafter to learn how he'd done it. He shared with me three prospecting rules that changed my efforts for good. I believe they will do the same for any salesperson. ■

1. *Never call on a prospect who isn't* **expecting** *your call*

2. *Never call on a prospect who isn't* **excited** *to talk to you*

3. *Never end a prospecting call without* **adding** *more value than you received*

Presentation isn't everything, but it is the *main thing.*

There's a restaurant in Minnesota called Kincaid's where the waiters know how to sell and the cooks deliver. Three friends and I were seated at a table there and before we had time to look over the menu, our waiter approached. His goal was simple.

He told us about the evening's special, the Kincaid Cut Prime Rib, juicy, three-inches thick and more tender than a stick of warm butter. To order it you had to say so then because it was in great demand and limited supply. It was the best thing they made, he admitted with pride, and by the way, wonderful with lobster. With that he left us to consider our options.

What options do you have when one makes that kind of offer? Anything that is not the Kincaid Cut Prime Rib is inferior. When the waiter returned, all four of us ordered the special, and, by the way, the lobster, too. None would miss out this night.

You can't build a sales business on presentation alone; but without it your sales business won't get built. Sure, if the cooks at Kincaid's had not delivered the juiciest, thickest, most savory prime rib we'd ever eaten, we would think twice about spending our money there again. But without the waiter's compelling presentation, few would experience the best the restaurant had to offer.

If your presentation isn't engaging, sensational, and set apart, then people will keep their options open. But when you tell them of a Kincaid Cut Prime Rib, their only choice is to miss out or dig in. ■

Make it so
their only choice
is to miss out
or dig in.

Prospecting begins by asking:
"Who do I know that knows who I want to know?"

Prospecting is a productivity game—not a numbers game. Your confidence and profits are only impacted positively by how many people say yes, not by how many calls you make. Therefore, to maximize your prospecting efficiency you should replace a more-is-better concept with a less-is-best strategy. In other words, you should spend less time cold-calling and more time going after warm prospects that are likely to say yes.

Most of us used this technique without knowing it. Perhaps you remember your first selling effort. Maybe it was cookies for Girl Scouts or magazines for school. My first recollection is selling candy for Little League at the age of eight. My dad told me that if I wanted to sell a lot I should go to people I knew and the people they knew. I took his advice and made a list which

included highlighting those I thought would buy the most. Within two days I was sold out when most of my teammates were just beginning.

Before you release an arrow at your prospecting target, it's important that you do all you can to increase your probability for success. That's obvious right? Yet most salespeople, I've found, overlook the most obvious place this should start … by asking the question: "Who do I know that knows who I want to know?" By answering this question you not only ascertain your most reliable prospecting sources, you also get help in your initial approach with prospects.

When you follow up on your list, don't just take names and numbers of prospects and move on. Ask the people you know to introduce you via email or phone or in person. I did this for my brother and he landed a lucrative account with the gentleman who sold me my car.

If you remember the maxim of social proof—that others can sell you better than you can sell yourself—this strategy make perfect sense. My dad was right. Asking the people you know to sell you to people they know is often the most productive method of prospecting there is. And as your clients grow to trust you as a friend, they too become people you know that know people you want to know. ■

Others can
sell you better
than you can
sell yourself.

Some customers aren't *worth it...* and they get in the way of those *who are.*

My approach to selling was simple: Get all the prospects you can, take all the business you can and make all the money you can. Using this can-do strategy, I managed to scare up a decent amount of business—it felt good. But then, sometime during my first year, I hit the ceiling of my potential. The phone was ringing off the hook and it wasn't new business. It was existing clients demanding special attention that I couldn't give them without ignoring someone else or putting off prospecting. Wanting to keep my job, I gave juggling a try. I employed a high-pressure approach to prospecting and a quick-fix approach to clients' problems. If I had five hands I may have pulled it off; but as it was I started dropping the ball. Rejections became routine and I received threats from current clients like, "If you can't do this, I'll take my business elsewhere." In response, I became a doormat for a while.

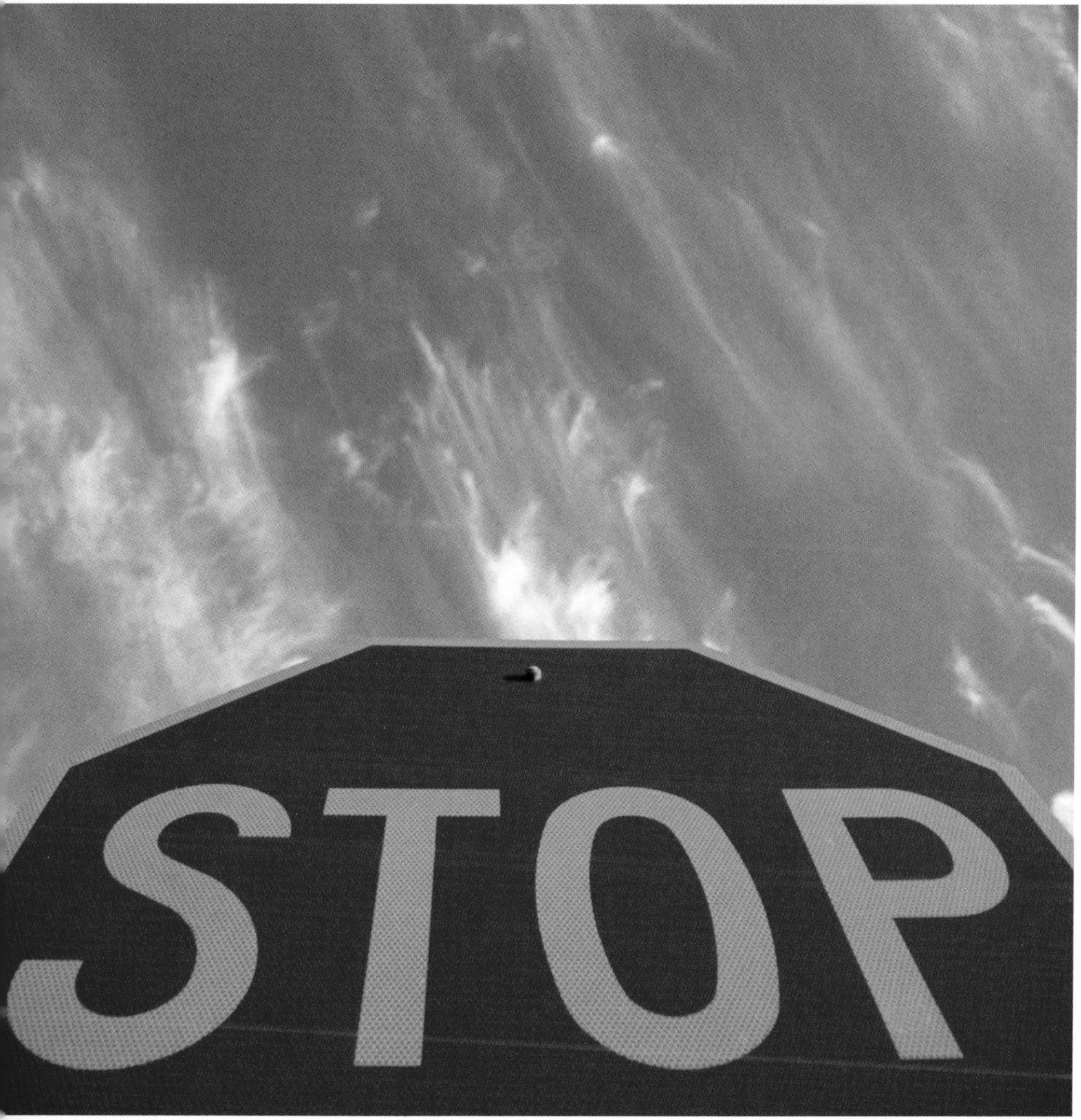
STOP

It was no way to make a living. Then one day it hit me like a foot in the face; the root of my problem wasn't me—it was the combination of me and my clients. Many of them did not share my ideals and values—things like integrity, courtesy and quality. They asked me to fudge numbers on contracts or ignore my other clients or complete tasks in an unreasonable amount of time. I paid closer attention and it was clear who was right for my business and who wasn't worth the time. This observation relieved me and scared me at the same time. But with some help from mentors I began excusing myself from the wrong relationships in order to free up more time for the right ones. I then changed the way I prospected. I prequalified potential customers with a planned interviewing process so that, at the outset of the relationship, I knew our values and expectations were aligned. This added two things to my sales approach: a higher degree of confidence and a lower degree of turnover. Before long my phone was ringing off the hook again—but this time it was the welcome sound of return and referral business. I learned that, when you rid your business of the wrong clients, you have time to take care of the right ones—and then they take care of you. ■

Your customers should share
*your **ideals and values,***
otherwise you're wasting
your time.

You'll have a
higher degree
of confidence
and a lower degree
of turnover.

Focus on the critical few...
not the insignificant many.

A customer *buys you first,* then your product.

Ask yourself a question and be honest with your answer. Would you buy from you? Think about how you approach a customer, the words you choose, your appearance, your mannerisms and your voice. If a salesperson just like you approached you in a store, would you take notice and listen? Or would you give a shrug off with, "I'm just looking?"

This isn't time for vain imaginations; the true impression you give customers is vital because you are part of your product—the first part, in fact. Often, if customers can't get past what they think of you, they won't even consider what you are offering.

On rare occasions customers will buy from people they are unimpressed and uncomfortable with; but if it happens, it typically happens only once. Customers who are turned off will rarely return to the same person, let alone refer their friends. Most buy from (and return to) people who make them comfortable. And they tell their friends about the experience. If your mannerisms, voice, approach and appearance are comforting, your customers will be more apt to listen to you; this is often your biggest selling hurdle.

Certainly, it is your first. ■

Would you buy from you?

*There are many areas that affect a customer's
initial impression of you, but here are four of the most important:*

■

Your non-verbal cues

*Are they welcoming and authentic or do they tip off that
you are in a hurry or have a selfish agenda?*

■

Your voice

*Do you speak in a humble-yet-confident tone or do you
sound apologetic and unsure of yourself?*

■

Your approach

*Do you introduce yourself and present a genuine,
value-adding proposition or do you default to ranting
about product or service features?*

■

Your appearance

*Does your appearance make your customers feel more or less
comfortable about dealing with you?*

Dialogue opens *doors.*

The best approaches to selling are aimed at relating not persuading. "The salesperson is not just an instrument of commerce," says Dr. William Isaacs, author of *Dialogue and the Art of Thinking Together* (Doubleday 1999), "but also an expert in human relations; and the rep's function is to make the customer feel better and understand better and feel more satisfied."

If the foundation of long-term success is dependable relationships, the goal of selling must be to establish trust. And that, says Dr. Isaacs, is the purpose of dialogue. There's more to it than two people in a conversation. "Dialogue," he explains, "is a conversation in which people think together in relationship.

Thinking together implies that you no longer take your own position as final. You relax your grip on certainty and listen to the possibilities that result from being in a relationship with others— possibilities that might not otherwise have occurred … Giving up trying to impose an agenda and genuinely listening to what is really needed and wanted in a situation is a far more potent way to operate."

To open doors that allow you to relate to your prospects on a level that will build trust (and subsequently close sales), you have to be willing to put your agenda on the back burner. You should facilitate conversation for the primary purpose of learning— knowing that this is the only way you can be certain to meet your customers needs and expectations. ■

Make
your customer
feel better,
understand better,
and feel more
satisfied.

Listen …
   opportunities
         are seldom labeled.

Advice is more important than *price.*

I t's usually the first thing to come up. "How much will it cost me?" asks the customer. We then dodge the question to avoid running them off before we have a chance to explain the value of the product.

Sure, there are those who pitch low prices and for them the price question is welcome. But regardless of where your price falls on the industry scale, it's not the cost that matters most to customers.

Consider one auto insurance's bold message to their potential customers: Call us and we'll give you our rates and the rates of five of our competitors—even if they are cheaper. What message does that send if you are thinking about buying auto insurance? For starters, it tells you

that the company is more interested in your satisfaction than in getting you to buy. Of course they don't want you to go to one of their competitors, but they're willing to bank on the fact that having a trustworthy insurance company is more important than a cheap one. So they're not afraid to offer you some helpful advice. "Here are your options," they say, "and we'll help advise you on which one is the best fit for your needs—even if that means introducing you to another company." It's an innovative way to highlight your intentions and, in the end, it builds trust.

There is always the chance you will lose a customer on price; but why not make it about more than price from the beginning. Offer them advice that indicates you care more about their overall satisfaction than their money. If they still choose a competitor after all, be ready when that other company falls short because you'll be the first person they call. And you won't have to prove yourself twice. ■

Offer customers advice.
That indicates you care
more about their overall satisfaction
than their money.

Everything
begins with an
idea.

Existing business is more *valuable* – and less stressful – than new business.

Most of us were given the impression that pursuing new business is the only way to increase profits. We were misled.

Your richest resource is people who already bought from you. Existing customers (I like to call them clients) have a history with you that makes them, one, more willing prospects, and two, more lucrative channels of marketing.

To be convinced enough to change the way you do business you have to understand the difference between a market-share mentality and a client-share mentality. A market-share mentality seeks to increase profits by selling to as many customers as possible in a given market, thus increasing one's

percentage of customers in that market. A client-share mentality seeks to increase profits by selling to existing clients and those they know, thus increasing one's percentage of business from each client. The cost comparison is telling.

A market-share mentality is a stressful strategy that relies on a constant influx of new business to maintain momentum. Prospecting remains necessary, as does outside marketing, since word-of-mouth is not reliable. Worse, seeking market-share spreads you thin and makes it increasingly difficult to maintain a high level of customer service (insert the "I'm just a number" feeling you get with many large companies who boast high market-share.)

On the flip-side, a client-share mentality steadily increases momentum without high reliance on cold-calling or outside marketing. Your investments focus on deepening relationships with existing clients and your prospecting banks on the maxim of social proof—that others can sell you better than you can sell yourself. Instead of drumming up new business you invest in referrals, which offer a much higher success rate. ■

Focus on
deepening relationships
with
existing clients
*instead of wasting
unnecessary time chasing
cold prospects.*

A customer
has
options;
you have
to be
different.

Two-thirds of sales customers continue to look for and purchase products from other vendors despite receiving the value and service they expected from their current vendor. This statistic indicates that meeting customers' expectations may be enough to close a sale, but it's not enough to keep a customer loyal.

In our marketplace of ever expanding choices, keeping clients takes more than courtesy, kindness and professionalism. You have to be different to keep consumers coming.

In their book *Differentiate or Die* (John Wiley & Sons, 2000), Jack Trout and Steve Rivkin cite the "explosion of choice" that has bombarded consumers since the 1970s. Vehicle models and styles have doubled. Soft drink brands have quadrupled. We once had sixteen types of bottled water to choose from and now we have fifty. Fifteen kinds of mouthwash wasn't enough so now we have sixty-six.

What about your market? How many options do your consumers have? If it follows the national trend, your consumers have more options than they probably realize—and it's just a matter of time before they discover another. If you are only giving them what they expect, you're not likely to have many loyal customers. It's true that you cannot stop offering good service and a quality product; but you must start offering something else, something that sets you apart. Ask yourself: What about me or my product makes me memorable? Then give your answer in how and what you sell. ∎

*You must start
offering something else,*

*something that
sets you apart.*

Salespeople
are
doctors,
not drug
dealers.

We go to doctors to rid ourselves of pain. We expect them to ask questions and prod us and ultimately to diagnose our problem and give us a solution. If a doctor walked in and, having never seen you before, said, "Okay, here's your prescription. Call me if you don't feel any better," you would be shocked. "Wait," you'd say. "How do you know this is what I need? You haven't even asked me what's wrong." Doctors rely on patients' input to diagnose and treat their problems. There is no other way they can carry out their job effectively.

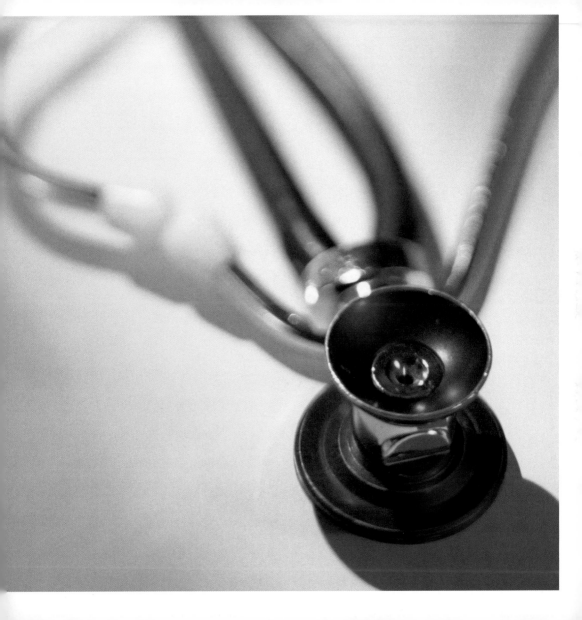

The drug-dealer's only challenge is to find the drug user. Once that's accomplished he doesn't need to ask questions or diagnose problems. People come to him because they want what he offers and he knows that he can charge any price he wants.

The salesperson stigma we all must overcome is a result of our colleagues (past and present) acting more like drug-dealers than doctors—assuming that all they need to do is find the right prospects and show up with the product in hand. If you are not diagnosing your customers' problems and assessing their needs before offering them a solution, you too are adding to the slimy salesperson stigma.

To rebrand society's view of salespeople, we'd all be wise to follow in the footsteps of the doctor. Question, assess, diagnose and prescribe. ■

Question.
  Assess.
    Diagnose.
      Prescribe.

Product knowledge is important, *people knowledge* is mandatory.

I was logging thousands of air miles a year, so my friend Mike offered to arrange a meeting with the owner of a travel agency. When the owner and I sat down I was eager to share my needs with him. I was not only looking for new ways to stretch my travel budget, I was also hoping for an innovative way to shrink my time on the road. My boys were growing up quickly.

The owner began with these words: "Todd, I'd like to tell you a little bit about our company," and away he went. He told me about the agency's history, the agency's reputation and why I should use the agency. He then showered me with features and benefits like the quarterly CD-ROM with listings of hotels and restaurants, the emergency hotline should I ever get stuck somewhere and, of course, an endless supply of luggage tags should I ever lose mine.

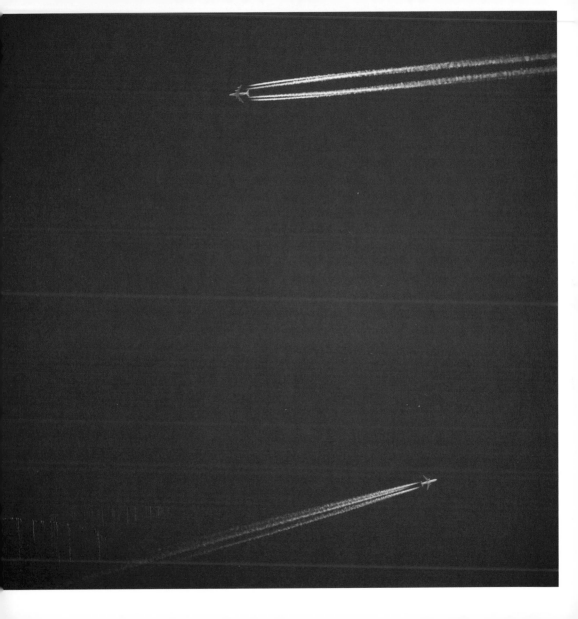

Then came the classic line: "Todd, we'd like to ask you for your business."

With my arms crossed I replied, "I'm not very motivated to give it to you."

"I could tell," he confessed.

I then asked him a series of questions. "What's my favorite airline? What's my favorite hotel? What time of day do I prefer to travel? Do I like staying near the airport or near my speaking venue? Do I like traveling on weekends? Does my family ever travel with me? Do I already own restaurant listings and luggage tags?"

The point was simple; he knew nothing about my personal values, my travel needs or my desires for a relationship with a travel agency. After a half-an-hour speech he knew nothing but my name. He started the meeting talking when he should have been listening. He knew everything about his product and nothing about me; and in the end he knew nothing he needed to know in order to close the sale.

Know your product well, but know your people better. ■

He knew *everything*
about his *product*,
but he knew *nothing*
about *me*.

He knew *nothing*
he needed to know to
close the sale.

People don't care
how much you know
until they know
how much
you care.

Training
doesn't matter
if you don't
build
trust.

Many sales managers get it wrong. They train their salespeople to close the deal but they never teach them how to get people interested in the offer.

The last two decades of sales training created the hill we climb today. Thanks largely to the hundreds of closing techniques that filled the pages of the sales books we read, the eighties and nineties taught us one thing: how to close. They never told us we had to build trust first. I think we're finally starting to learn.

Trust is the language of successful relationships—including sales relationships—and a common language is necessary for two people to communicate in the most effective manner. You know this firsthand if you've ever visited a foreign country and asked for directions. You probably made a lot of hand gestures and exaggerated facial expressions to convey your point. The same dynamic occurs between you and a customer if you don't speak the language of trust.

If you're speaking in the language of Hurry-Up-and-Buy or Need-to-Meet-My-Quota, customers won't get you. It doesn't matter how well you speak it or how many props you use; you are still speaking in a foreign dialect that generally initiates frustration.

On the other hand, when you communicate in Trust, putting their needs first and demonstrating a genuine desire to help, customers reply in Trust through positive responses—repeat sales and solid referrals. And remember, to retain fluency in any language you must not only master it, you must also use it regularly. ■

Gaining

trust

is

like

filling

a

bucket

one

drop

at

a

time.

Sustained sales success takes a team.

Most salespeople spend eighty-percent of their time completing menial tasks that have no bearing on the bottom line.

We've been bred to pull up our own bootstraps each morning; and yes our boots were made for forging new territory and treading the competition. But there's only so much we can do in one pair of boots.

Several years ago I was the president, accountant, sales rep, marketing exec, speaker and writer of my company. It was growing at a modest rate of 2.5 percent a year. Then a friend told me the truth and immediately I changed my shoes.

My boots were too heavy, he said, like concrete galoshes. My progress was never going to improve if I didn't lighten the load. In short, he was telling me I was a control freak—the only one I trusted—and I was a burden on myself. I couldn't do it all, he insisted. I needed to figure out what I did best and delegate the rest.

He is right. One is too small a number in order to achieve greatness. There will come a point in every progressive sales career when a team is not only necessary to keep up with business, it is also mandatory for continued success.

I gave up my jobs as president, accountant, sales rep, marketing exec and writer to people far more capable than I, and the company began to flourish at a rate of 40 percent a year. In fact, a few months ago, the same friend and I shared a game of golf and he told me he was scaling back some more of his responsibility. He asked me a question. Would I be interested in buying his company? I was. ■

1

*is too small
a number*

*to achieve
greatness.*

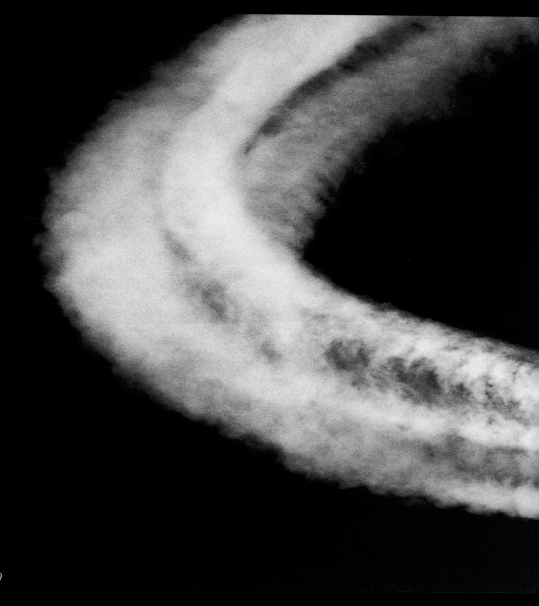

Teamwork
makes the
dream work.

Partnerships *fortify* a sales business.

Knowing your clients better than the competition is your only insurance against loss of business. To maintain this edge you must move your relationships beyond the boundaries of a buyer-seller affiliation to a place of partnership governed by give and take. In other words, to keep clients, you must get them involved. But as you know from your non-work relationships, give and take rarely happens without effort.

Your clients' motivation to give you repeat and referral business is largely a function of your initiation and leadership. You must give them reason to invest in the relationship. There are a number of strategies for accomplishing this, but they all lead back to one activity: ongoing communication.

Strategies for initiating this will remain as plentiful as marketing trends, but the most transcendent is co-creation, a.k.a. letting your clients take part in defining the product or service they purchase.

In their November 2004 newsletter, Trendwatching.com dubs this "Customer-Made" and defines it as the strategy of market-mindful corporations to create "goods, services and experiences in close cooperation with consumers, tapping into their intellectual capital, and in exchange giving them a direct say in what actually gets produced, manufactured, developed, designed, serviced, or processed." Exhibit A: Apple's iPodlounge.com where iPod users can congregate to discuss their favorite features and relay what they'd like the next iPod to do. The site gets more than 5 million hits a day. Exhibit B: Niketalk.com, an online community whose sister site NikeChat invites Nike fans every Sunday evening to exchange views, thoughts and tips. According to Trendwatching.com, there have been more than 3.5 million posts thus far.

Such tools make ongoing conversation not only fun but fiscally wise. The premise is simple; the more involved clients are, the more loyal they become. When you can initiate and foster partnerships like these, you add years to the life of your business. Isn't stability what you really want after all? ∎

The
more involved
clients are,
the more loyal
they become.

If you
  don't put
boundaries
    on your
  business,
you will
    never achieve
balance
  in your life.

I doubt any of us would trade the life we ultimately desire for more business. And I'm certain that you would not rather be working late hours than enjoying an evening with people you love. Yet, in more than two decades of selling and sales training, I've known more salespeople to make those trade-offs than not.

I watched one put on pound after quiet pound while putting in his time. I noticed another cancel a family vacation to meet with a prospect. I witnessed another lose the love of her life while getting ahead. Would they have done what they did had they known the outcome? Never. They just thought a different outcome would occur.

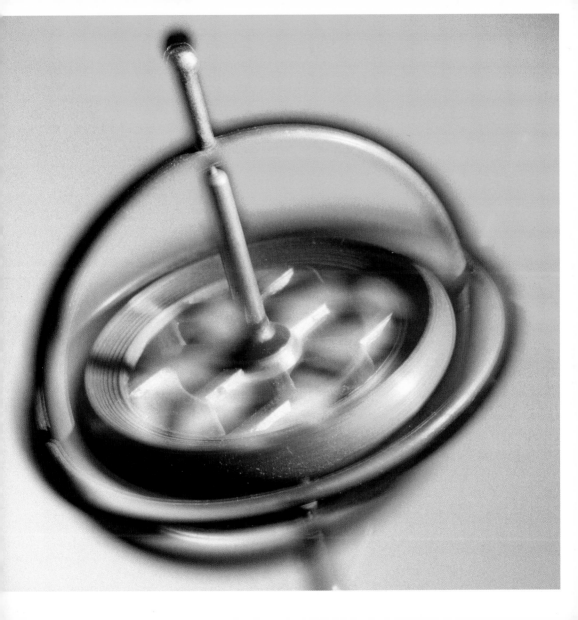

I've seen more collateral damage from selling than you can imagine and I have a feeling that's because most salespeople think that sales success requires life sacrifice. The trouble is that it's the other way around. To be successful in life, you must make sacrifices at work.

Think about it; isn't success in any endeavor a matter of upholding your priorities? By definition success should produce more life satisfaction, right? Your sales career, then, if it is successful, should produce more of what you want from life. We tend to forget this. We tend to subscribe to the notion that business and pleasure are two separate pursuits. The truth is that business should be a part of and party to pleasure. In other words, selling and living should complement each other. Only when that is true are you truly successful. And that only happens when you put boundaries on your pursuit of more business in order to maintain time for more life. ◼

To be
successful in life,
you must make
sacrifices at work.

The most important sale is the one you make to *yourself.*

Why are you selling? Better yet, why did you choose the sales profession in the first place? Your answers are critical to your success—and here's why.

If you don't know why you sell—if you don't know your deepest motivation for offering your product or service—you will never make it through the tough times. And they will come.

Sales can be a roller coaster of a career. Peaks and valleys. Highs and lows. Yeses and Nos. I'm sure you've already experienced the ride. But to continue on this undulating journey requires something more than a strong stomach. It requires heart.

Reaching the peaks is fun, but your memory fades quickly in the shadowed valleys. And valleys require heart. Succeeding over the long-haul requires a deeper passion about why you do what you do.

So now let's ask: Why do you sell? What is your deeper motive? What keeps you going when the going is standing still? What gets you up in the morning when the sales sun hasn't risen in several weeks?

Providing for your family? That's a good motive, but go deeper. What about the selling business do you love? Serving people? Making people's lives a little better than they were before they met you? Fulfilling people's dreams? Those will get you up in the morning.

Whatever your deepest motive is, you must know it; that's the point. And you must remind yourself of it regularly—in the good times and especially in the bad. Because when your core motive is clear and constantly in mind, you are able to sell yourself on selling every day. ■

*To continue
on this*
undulating
journey
requires
heart.

Wherever you go,
go there with
all your heart.

Making a *difference* is more important than making a dollar.

The person who interviewed you for your first sales position probably asked something like, "Why do you want this job?" Think back. What was your response? Certainly you didn't say something like, "Because I want to get rich and buy lots of nice things." You were probably more clever than that.

Chances are, your answer had something to do with "great opportunity" and "high potential." But what else did you say? I'd lay a bet you were smart enough to mention that you "liked helping people" or something to that effect. Isn't that the answer we're supposed to give—whether or not we mean it?

Why, on our best-foot-forward, interview-ready behavior, do we think we need to mention that we enjoy helping other people? Do we think it just sounds good or do we, deep down, understand that helping other people is truly the highest calling of the sales profession?

Even though we often forget, we acknowledge it: making a difference is more important than making a dollar. Sure, a dollar puts food on the table and a roof over our head and four shiny wheels in the garage, but we know in our gut that more money won't matter as much in the end. What will matter are the people whose lives we touched along the way. Money provides outward pleasure and that's a fair reward for being good at what we do. But making a difference fulfills you in a way that money can't.

And here's the beauty of this truth: When people take precedence over profits, profits begin to climb. People like doing business with salespeople who care more about them than their bank accounts. ■

How many lives
will you touch
along the way?

About Todd Duncan

For over two decades, Todd Duncan has been a friend and mentor to millions of ambitious professionals worldwide. Since the age of twenty-three he has lived in the trenches and knows what it takes to succeed amidst the rising pressures and incessant temptations of the marketplace. It is from this platform that he teaches and touches the lives of some 300,000 professionals every year.

Inc., CNN Money, SUCCESS, Fox Business, Investor's Business Daily, Entrepreneur, and Washington Business Journal are just a short sampling of the numerous media outlets who have featured Duncan's material. As an author, his books have landed on prestigious bestseller lists including the New York Times, Los Angeles Times, Wall Street Journal, Barnes & Noble, Amazon.com, CEOread.com, and BusinessWeek and are now in 30 languages world-wide.

Todd's Journey

Todd has always been highly motivated but his ambition didn't at first lead to true success. By the age of 27, he was listed in the top one-percent of his industry, earning hundreds of thousands a year but his world was dangerously out of balance. Eventually, his personal empire of expensive toys and fast living was toppled by a two-year cocaine addiction. On his way down, he faced up to his shortcomings and thus embarked on a road to recovery and redemption.

Through the support of friends and mentors like John Maxwell, Zig Ziglar, Og Mandino and Ken Blanchard, Todd not only recovered but quickly re-ascended to the top. At thirty he founded his first training company and began researching successful people in all walks of business and life. Over the past two decades, Todd has built a respected worldwide enterprise while continuing to observe and study the lives of achievers who thrive on and off the job. His ongoing discoveries are synthesized into compelling resources for living in a meaningful, enriching and profitable way. His best-selling books and popular seminars have influenced millions to pursue a generous and abundant life.

Todd's Content

Todd's blockbuster title, High Trust Selling, has revolutionized the mindset of the sales industry. Resulting from over twenty years of market research and analysis, the book unpacks proven principles by which salespeople can establish long-lasting and high-yielding bonds of trust with their clients. In High Trust Selling, Todd distills these principles into fourteen clear-cut laws. The book has been lauded as required reading for professionals around the globe and has become a cornerstone resource of numerous corporations.

Todd's next blockbuster, Time Traps, made the New York Times bestseller six weeks after its release. In it, Duncan offers proven remedies for being swamped and reveals how to set a schedule that works every day. The principles in Time Traps have been hailed as a revolutionary that finally teaches professionals how to boost their careers while decreasing their work hours and make more money in the process.

Todd's Company

In 1992, Todd founded The Duncan Group to meet the growing demand for innovative training and leadership in the mortgage banking industry where he began his career. In subsequent years, The Duncan Group has expanded its scope of operations to influence the general market and has earned its reputation as one of the elite personal development companies in the world.

Captivating as a speaker and author and admired as a leader, Todd Duncan's passion is to unlock the potential in every individual crossing his path. In designing world-renowned content and universal success strategies, Todd's ultimate goal is to help people lead healthy lives of fulfillment and satisfaction.

Todd and his two sons live in Newport Beach, California.

You can contact Todd Duncan at:

Todd Duncan The Duncan Group(858) 551-0920 Officewww.toddduncan.com

If you have enjoyed this book we invite you to check out our entire collection of gift books, with free inspirational movies, at **www.simpletruths.com.** You'll discover it's a great way to inspire *friends* and *family,* or to thank your best *customers* and *employees.*

For more information, please visit us at:
www.simpletruths.com Or call us toll free... **800-900-3427**